To my mother for her wisdom that brought magic to my childhood, and to my son who taught me what fun it is to be a mother, and to all the others in my "human family," especially Olly, Judy, and Audrey.

Jane Goodall

National Geographic Learning | Cengage Learning

1 Lower Ragsdale Drive
Building 1, Suite 200
Monterey, CA 93940

Visit National Geographic Learning online at **NGL.Cengage.com**
Visit our corporate website at www.cengage.com

Printed in the United States of America
Quad Graphics, Leominster, MA

ISBN: 978-1-133-89970-9

19 20 21 22

11 10 9 8 7 6

Jane Goodall **The Chimpanzee Family Book**

with photographs by Michael Neugebauer

NATIONAL GEOGRAPHIC

This wild and beautiful country is part of Gombe National Park in Tanzania, East Africa. It is the country I love most in the world, the home of the wild chimpanzees.

For nearly 30 years I have lived and worked among these amazing creatures who are so nearly human. In the 30 square miles (80 square kilometers) of the park there are about 150 chimpanzees living in three separate communities. Each community has about 50 members.

It is an hour since I left my little house and climbed into the hills to search for chimpanzees. I heard some calling early in the morning, but this small group is the first I have found.

Once you get used to them, each chimpanzee looks quite different from every other, just as we do. I have given names to all the chimpanzees I know, and chimpanzees in the same family have names that start with the same letter.

This is Gremlin. She is 18 years old. Hidden in her lap, protected by her encircling arms, her small baby is sleeping. Gremlin is a wonderful mother. She is gentle, affectionate, and playful. Her baby is called Galahad and he is five months old.

Every day when I am at Gombe, I follow a different chimp. Today I shall stay with Gremlin and her infant until dusk, writing down all that they do. The writing is important because I have made the scientific study of chimpanzees my life's work, and scientists must keep careful records.

When little Galahad wakes up, Gremlin grooms him with gentle, caressing movements of her fingers. Loving this attention, he is quite relaxed.

Right now Gremlin is with her two brothers. Goblin, the eldest of the family, is 24 years old. He is the big boss, the number-one male, respected by all the other members of his community—6 other adult males and 32 females and youngsters. Goblin got to this position of power not because of his size— he is small—but because he was absolutely determined to get to the top. Since chimpanzees live to be 40 to 50 years old, Goblin is in the prime of his life. Gimble, aged 11 years, hero-worships his powerful brother and often follows him on his travels through the forest.

Galahad finds his two grown-up uncles fascinating. He watches them, constantly learning.

Suddenly as I watch Galahad, I see his eyes open wide and he gives a little call, "o—o—o," of surprise. Goblin is staring in the same direction and his hair begins to bristle.

All at once Goblin charges towards an adult male who has appeared at the edge of the clearing. Goblin stamps the ground, hits on tree trunks, and hurls a rock. He leaps up and shakes the vegetation. All these things make him look very large and fierce. This was how he challenged the other males when he was working his way to the top position. It is called the charging display.

The newcomer is my long-time friend Evered, the oldest of the Gombe chimpanzees. He is about 38 years old. Then I hear rustling in the dry grass. A stick snaps. I know that other chimpanzees are approaching this quiet place. Goblin charge towards them and they rush out of his way. Some climb into the trees. There is much calling and screaming.

During the excitement one of the young males is seized and pounded on the ground. Although this fight looks very fierce and brutal, the victim is not hurt. But he screams very loudly indeed and this adds to the commotion.

Finally, having made sure that all the other chimps are properly respectful of him, Goblin calms down.

Then the victim of the fight approaches Goblin and crouches low like someone wanting to be forgiven—even though he had done no wrong. He is soon calmed by the gentle touch of Goblin's hand.

Other chimps climb down from the trees. Gremlin greets one of the adult males with a kiss, and then little Galahad greets him too and is embraced.

Now that the excitement is over, the chimps settle down and start to groom each other. Grooming is a very important activity for them. It helps to keep their coats clean. And it helps them to be more relaxed and friendly with each other.

It is amazing to see how quickly a frightened or hurt chimp is calmed when a companion grooms him. Goblin, the most important male, gets a lot of attention from the others.

After grooming each other for about an hour, the chimps decide it is time to move on. The hot, lazy midday rest period is over. Goblin leads the way down the slope into the forest. Gremlin gets up and follows along behind.

For a while Galahad clings to Gremlin's belly, but then he begins to scramble up onto her back. He is only just learning how to do this and he has quite a struggle to get up there. When he finally makes it, he looks rather unsafe and soon he begins to slip.

Then Gremlin stops and firmly puts her son back underneath. He stays there for a few minutes. But then he again clambers up onto her back. She has to keep stopping to settle him, and we fall far behind the others.

In the forest it is cool and dim after the heat and brightness of the open hillside. There is a clear, fast-flowing mountain stream in the valley and Gremlin pauses to drink, sucking the water up with her lips. Galahad is fascinated by this strange silvery liquid. It seems to run past so quickly, yet it never goes away.

I love to be along with the chimps in the forest. With no humans to distract me
I can feel a part of the cool, quiet green world with its flashes of bright color, and
I can listen to the rustling of the leaves and the sounds of the birds and insects.

With sudden soft grunts of pleasure Gremlin climbs to feed on little green figs. She crunches loudly and goes on making small sounds of pleasure.

Galahad reaches to touch the fruits, keeping close to his mother. He has only four teeth and won't start eating any solid foods for several months. And even then, milk will remain his most important food until he is about three years old.

Nearby another group of chimps is feeding. We hear their calls of delight as they too feast on figs. Sometimes Gremlin replies with contented sounds of her own, as though to say, "I have delicious food too."

After stuffing herself with fruit for over an hour, Gremlin moves on and climbs up into more open country.

Suddenly she stops and peers through the undergrowth ahead. There are three chimpanzees sitting quietly together. Gremlin obviously sees who they are before I do, for she soon relaxes and moves on again.

As we get closer, I too recognize Fifi with two members of her family. Fifi is my oldest chimpanzee friend at Gombe. I first knew her when she was two years old. Now she is 29 and has four offspring of her own. With her today are her two daughters, four-year-old Flossi, and Fanni, who is nine.

As Gremlin approaches, she gives a grunt of greeting, then sits in the shade. Fifi gives a soft grunt in reply.

After a few minutes Flossi and Fannie start to play. Fifi can't resist joining in. She tickles Flossi with her fingers and nibbles into her neck. Flossi laughs louder and louder. Chimp laughing doesn't sound exactly like ours, but it is pretty much the same. Certainly we know exactly what the breathy, grunting chuckles mean.

Fifi has always been very playful. That was especially lucky for her first infant, because he, of course, had no brothers or sisters to play with when he was small. Fifi plays with her daughters for five minutes and then relaxes as the two girls romp beside her.

Galahad very carefully climbs a little way up a sapling close to his mother. He dangles from a small branch, reaching playfully to Gremlin. Occasionally she pats at him gently so that his mouth opens wide in a playface.

As he dangles there, Galahad is watching Flossi and Fanni. In a few months he will be old enough to join in the games of other youngsters. They will be delighted, for young chimps love to play with very small infants. But even though they will play very gently with him, his mother will watch carefully and snatch her precious infant away if his playmates get even the tiniest bit rough. And if they accidently hurt him and make him scream, Gremlin will threaten or even hit them.

Now the game is over, and Flossi starts to suckle. She will not be able to do this for many more months. Fifi's milk is drying up and she often prevents Flossi from nursing these days. Then Flossi pouts and utters sad crying sounds until Fifi relents and lets her suckle for just a little while. In about a year Fifi will probably have another infant. Then Flossi will be able to play with and carry the baby just as her own big sister Fanni did with her.

When Flossi wakes from her nap, she spies a hard-shelled fruit lying on the ground. She picks it up and tries to crack it open against a tree trunk. But Fifi notices and at once snatches the fruit for herself. Flossi watches as her mother hits the fruit four times against a rock, splits the shell, and begins to feed.

Fifi often sits staring into space, seeming to daydream. I always wonder what she is thinking. Chimpanzees certainly do think.

They are always having to make decisions, such as what to do next, or where to go, or whom to spend time with. Do they also think about things that have happened to them, or things they would like to happen? I suspect they do.

Meanwhile Fanni has taken a couple of bananas from my pocket. I was planning to put medicine in them for one of the chimps who is sick. But I have not seen him today. Fanni is obviously enjoying her stolen meal.

It is Flossi who is the first to climb into a nearby tree. But she does so only when she has made certain that Fifi is following. Mother and daughter feed on young leaf buds. Fanni feeds in another tree a bit further away.

Half an hour later Flossi after her meal of frigs and leaf buds, is well content. Relaxed and comfortable, she seems to be daydreaming too.

Suddenly Flossi sits upright and stares towards a palm tree about 70 feet (20 meters) away. I look too, and see Frodo, her 12-year-old brother.

Frodo is feeding on the pith of one of the palm fronds. The fronds are tough and it is hard work tearing them apart. Once the job is done, the length of white pith looks rather like sugar cane. Frodo crunches it up and sucks the juices out. When all the goodness has gone, he will spit out the fibers that remain.

When chimps eat palm pith, it always looks so delicious-and I'm sure it is, for them. But I found it very disappointing when I tried it myself. It is hard and tough and has almost no taste at all.

After a while Frodo climbs down. His elder brother, Freud, appears. Freud is 17. He has also been feeding in a nearby palm. The brothers are very close friends and often help each other.

When Frodo was an infant, he used to watch everything that Freud did. Often he would try to imitate what he saw. Once, for example, when Frodo was one and a half years old, he watched as Freud leapt up and hit and kicked a tree trunk, making a drumming sound. Chimps often do this when they are traveling. Frodo, who was still very unsteady on his feet, tried to do the same. He lost his balance, tumbled down a slope, and had to be rescued by his mother. But a few days later he tried again, most successfully. In this way he learned to do many things at a much younger age than most infants.

The first time Freud left his mother to travel for a few days with the big males, he was eight years old, but Frodo sometimes left Fifi when he was only five. He did so only when he was with his big brother. He knew he could run to Freud for help and comfort if things went wrong.

These days Freud is very wary of Goblin, who has attacked him a few times. Goblin knows Freud would like to take over the top position. But Freud is not yet confident enough to stand up to Goblin, so he often avoids him and travels by himself. Sometimes Frodo keeps him company, as he is doing today. And now it is Freud who seems to get comfort from the presence of his brother.

After his meal Freud relaxes. Carefully he grooms himself, then yawns as he grows drowsy.

Of course there are other animals at Gombe besides the chimpanzees. There are a few leopards, some bushbucks, and bushpigs, and several different kinds of monkeys. And there are very many baboons.

The baboons travel around in troops of about 50. The chimpanzees meet at least one of these troops every day.

Even though they eat mostly plant foods, chimpanzees are sometimes hunters, and seem to enjoy eating meat. They prey on young animals, especially young monkeys. And sometimes they hunt infant baboons, but not very often because it is dangerous. Adult male baboons have huge canine teeth, and they quickly join forces to protect a young baboon who is in danger.

Mostly, though, the chimps and the baboons share the forests peacefully together. Young chimps and young baboons may even play with each other.

For the past hour the sounds of baboons down in the valley have been coming closer. Now, at about four o'clock, the troop is all around us.

Suddenly Flossi bounces towards a young male baboon about the same size as herself. She pats playfully towards him. Seizing her back, he makes biting, tickling movements around her shoulders. Then he rolls her over and bites into her tummy.

Galahad watches Flossi and the baboon. He is far too young for such play. Even if he tried to join in, Gremlin would prevent him.

After about ten minutes Flossi bounces away from her baboon friend. Fifi is leaving and her daughters both follow. Flossi scampers after her mother and jumps onto her back, perching there like a small jockey.

Gremlin moves off also, but she goes in a different direction. Soon she moves into some very thick vegetation. I have to crawl on my hands and knees. I keep getting tangled in the vines, and thorns catch my clothes and skin. Gremlin moves easily through this tangle, Galahad clinging to her belly. I lose sight of her.

Suddenly I see a chimpanzee sitting in a little clearing. Ah! I think this must be Gremlin. But when I emerge from the undergrowth, I find that it is not. It is Wunda with her little brother Wolfi. She has her arm protectively around him. Where is their mother? They have no mother, these two. She died five months ago. And so Wunda, nine and a half years old, is caring for her small brother. She lets him ride on her back and share her sleeping nest at night. She does her best to be a real mother to him.

Little chimps are always very dependent upon their mothers. Over the years at Gombe I have known other instances where infants were so upset when they lost their mothers that, even though they had older brothers or sisters to care for them, they fell sick and died.

Wolfi is unhappy too. But even before his mother died, he had spent a lot of time with Wunda, feeding close beside her and often riding on her back when the family traveled. Now she is helping him to get over his grief.

When Wunda climbs to feed, Wolfi follows quickly. But he gets left behind as they climb the tall tree trunk. He gives soft, sad cries and Wunda stops and reaches back to help him.

Up in the tree Wunda sits, looking around for the best place to feed. Wolfi sits close to her. You can see the sad, sad expression in his eyes.

I am still hoping to find Gremlin and Galahad, so I leave Wunda and Wolfi and move on. Presently I see another chimpanzee ahead. But again it is not Gremlin. This is Wilkie – elder brother of Wunda and Wolfi. He is 16, one year younger than Freud.

Wilkie is feeding on termites. He is using a grass stem as a tool to fish them from their underground nest. He pushed the stem carefully down one of the tunnels into the hard clay of the termite mound, leaves it there for a moment, then slowly pulls it out. Many termites are clinging to the grass stem with their jaws. Wilkie picks them off with his lips, one by one, and scrunches them. Then he fishes again. Chimps use other objects as tools too. They use sticks to fish for fierce, biting army ants, and crumpled leaves for sopping up water from hollows in tree trunks where rainwater has gathered which they cannot reach with their lips. Also the chimps sometimes use rocks and branches as weapons, to throw and to club.

I leave Wilkie to his fishing and go on, still searching for Gremlin. I am lucky, for some ten minutes later I come across her sitting on the ground. From time to time she gazes around the trees above. She is probably looking for a good patch of food.

Galahad is chewing on the end of a dry stick. First he looks thoughtful, even a bit sad. And then most determined look comes into his eyes.

Already, at only five months old, Galahad has a strong personality and a mind of his own. One day, I feel sure, that this little chimp will become the top male of his community. He has such good care from his mother. And he has such a good example to follow because his uncle, Goblin, is top male now.

Finally Gremlin makes up her mind. She climbs into a fig tree and starts her last meal of the day.

It is getting dusk now, and Galahad is a very small black silhouette against the evening sky. As I sit and watch him, I hear chimps calling nearby. There is a group feeding on leaf buds, probably Fifi with some of her family-perhaps Wunda and little Wolfi, too.

Gremlin replies to the calls. These are beautiful calls, like singing. The chimpanzees make these sounds only when they are well content, well fed, at the end of the day. "Seven o'clock on a fine summer evening," they seem to call out, "and all's well with the world."

I leave them there, for it is nearly dark and I have some way to go. They will make their sleeping nests close by, so I shall be able to find them in the morning. As I hurry down the mountainside towards my little house on the shore of Lake Tanganyika, I hear again the melodious singing calls. And I hear other voices joined to the chorus, from further south. Goblin, too, is calling his "good night."

These chimpanzees, living in a national park, are lucky. It is not so good for those in other parts of Africa. In many places the forests where chimps once lived have been felled for timber, or to make space for houses or crops. In some places where chimps remain they are hunted for food. Often mothers are shot and their infants taken. These infants are sold to zoos and circuses, for pets, and for medical research. It is terrible, and cruel, and some nights I cannot sleep for thinking of it all, and planning ways to try to help the chimpanzees.

But at least in Tanzania the chimpanzees are well protected. FIfi and her family, Wilkie, Wunda, and Wolfi, Evered and Goblin, Gremlin and little Galahad—and all the others too—are safe from humans. They have learned to trust us—and we must never let them come to harm at our hands.

Tonight, as I lie listening to the lapping of the lake on the shore, my mind will be filled with pictures of little Galahad.